The Art of Garlic Farming

A Practical Guide to Growing and
Selling Garlic for Profit

Introduction

Garlic has been cultivated for centuries, not only for its distinctive flavour and culinary uses but also for its remarkable health benefits. Known as the "stinking rose," garlic has found its way into the hearts and kitchens of countless food lovers around the world. But what if we told you that garlic is not only a delicious ingredient but also a lucrative crop that could turn your passion for farming into a profitable venture?

Welcome to "The Art of Garlic Farming: A Practical Guide to Growing and Selling Garlic for Profit." In this comprehensive and enthralling guide, we will delve into the world of garlic cultivation, unravelling the secrets to successful garlic farming and sharing invaluable insights that can help you establish a thriving garlic farm.

Garlic farming is not just an ordinary agricultural pursuit; it is an art form that requires patience, knowledge, and meticulous attention to detail. It is a delicate dance between the forces of nature and the skill of the farmer. The journey begins with selecting the right garlic varieties, understanding the soil requirements, and preparing the land to create the perfect environment for garlic to flourish.

As you embark on this farming adventure, you will discover the wealth of benefits that garlic farming holds. Apart from its market demand and profitability, garlic farming offers a multitude of advantages. It is a sustainable practice that promotes healthy soil management, requires fewer chemical interventions, and contributes to a greener and more environmentally responsible agricultural sector.

Join us as we explore the intricacies of each stage of garlic farming, from pre-planting preparation to harvesting and storage. Understand the importance of soil testing, optimal planting techniques, and best practices for soil nutrient management. Conquer the challenges of weed and pest control, and learn how to protect your garlic crop from diseases that can jeopardize your harvest.

But garlic farming isn't just about nurturing the plants; it's also about understanding the market and effectively selling your prized crop. In this guide, we will equip you with the knowledge to identify your target market, establish direct connections with consumers and retailers, and even explore the world of online sales and marketing.

As we venture deeper into the art of garlic farming, you will gain insights into the potential for expansion and scaling up your garlic production. Discover strategies for diversification, managing labour and equipment on a larger scale, and long-term planning that can optimize your profitability and ensure the sustainability of your garlic farm.

Whether you are a novice farmer seeking to embark on a new agricultural adventure or an experienced grower looking to diversify your crop portfolio, "The Art of Garlic Farming" is the essential guide that will empower you to unlock the immense potential of garlic cultivation. Get ready to immerse yourself in the world of garlic farming, where science and passion harmoniously intertwine to create not just a sustainable agricultural venture but a pathway to culinary delight and financial success.

Are you ready to embark on this extraordinary journey into the enchanting world of garlic farming? Let us delve into the secrets and intricacies of this ancient crop with its vibrant history and promising future. Prepare to cultivate the stinking rose and turn your passion into profit.

Chapter One

Introduction to Garlic Farming

1.1 Importance of Garlic Farming

Garlic (Allium sativum) has been cultivated for thousands of years across the globe for its culinary and medicinal properties. Garlic is a member of the onion family, and it has a unique flavour and aroma that have made it a well-established ingredient in recipes around the world. It is also known for its health-promoting properties, which have sparked interest in its cultivation and consumption in recent years.

Garlic farming holds considerable importance today for various reasons, including its economic and health benefits. Garlic is a high-value crop, and its global production and consumption have been significantly increasing in recent years, creating a thriving market for this crop. The increasing demand for garlic has opened up avenues for farmers to tap into this market and contribute to the global economy.

Moreover, garlic has several health benefits that have been widely recognized in the scientific community. Garlic is rich in vitamins and minerals, including vitamin C, vitamin B6, and manganese, among others. It also contains allicin, a sulfur-containing compound that is responsible for its pungent odor and has potent antioxidant and anti-inflammatory properties. Studies have suggested that garlic consumption can help reduce the risk of various chronic illnesses, including heart diseases, cancer, and diabetes.

Garlic farming also plays a significant role in sustainable agriculture. Garlic is an excellent crop to rotate with other crops, and this rotation helps improve soil health by reducing soil-borne diseases, pests, and pathogens. Furthermore, garlic farming can promote biodiversity if done sustainably, creating a habitat for beneficial insects.

In addition to its health and economic benefits, garlic holds cultural significance in many regions across the world. Garlic has been used in traditional medicine and religious practices and is an essential ingredient in many cultural cuisines. Its cultural significance has helped preserve its legacy and kept the demand for garlic high even in the face of international competition.

Lastly, garlic is a relatively easy crop to grow, making it attractive to small farmers and even home gardeners. Garlic cultivation requires little input other than preparing the soil, planting, and periodic care, making it relatively low maintenance. Garlic farming can provide smallholder farmers with a livelihood, and its high value means that it can be sold for a reasonable price, generating revenue and creating a sustainable income stream.

In conclusion, Garlic farming has significant importance today, including its economic, health, environmental, and cultural benefits. The increasing demand for garlic worldwide, accompanied by its well-documented health benefits and cultural significance, has made it an essential crop for farmers to consider. Despite its specific requirements for soil preparation and climate, garlic farming is relatively easy, making it accessible to smallholder farmers and home gardeners alike. Garlic farming is an excellent opportunity for farmers to embrace sustainable agriculture, maintain their livelihoods, and contribute to global food security.

1.2 Benefits of Garlic Farming

Garlic farming offers a multitude of benefits, not only for farmers but also for consumers, the environment, and the overall agricultural sector. From its nutritional value to its economic and environmental advantages, garlic farming has become an attractive venture. Let's delve into the various benefits of garlic farming:

1. Nutritional Value and Health Benefits

Garlic is renowned for its numerous health benefits. It is a nutrient-dense crop, rich in vitamins, minerals, antioxidants, and bioactive compounds. Regular consumption of garlic has been associated with various health advantages, including:

- Cardiovascular Health: Garlic has been shown to help lower blood pressure, reduce cholesterol levels, and contribute to overall cardiovascular health. Its compounds may help prevent the formation of blood clots and promote healthy blood circulation.

- Antibacterial and Antifungal Properties: Garlic contains compounds with potent antibacterial and antifungal properties that can help fight off various infections. It has been used traditionally as a natural remedy for common ailments, such as colds and coughs.

- Anticancer Potential: Studies suggest that garlic may have anticancer properties, with the potential to inhibit the growth of cancer cells and reduce the risk of certain types of cancers, including stomach, colon, and breast cancer.

- Immune System Boost: Garlic can strengthen the immune system, helping to ward off illnesses and infections. Its immunomodulatory properties support the body's defense mechanisms and promote overall well-being.

2. Economic Opportunities

Garlic farming presents an excellent opportunity for farmers to diversify their crops and potentially increase their income. The market demand for garlic has been steadily growing, both locally and globally, contributing to its economic significance. The high value and relatively low production costs of garlic make it an attractive crop for farmers, particularly small-scale farmers who can cultivate garlic on smaller plots of land. The profitability of garlic farming can provide farmers with greater financial stability and potentially open doors to new markets and customers.

3. Sustainable Agriculture

Garlic farming aligns well with the principles of sustainable agriculture, fostering environmentally responsible farming practices. Some of the sustainability benefits of garlic farming include:

- Crop Rotation: Garlic is an excellent rotation crop, helping break pest and disease cycles, reducing the need for chemical interventions, and improving soil health and fertility.

- Reduced Chemical Use: Garlic farming often requires fewer chemical inputs compared to other crops, especially when managed properly. This reduces the environmental impact and promotes healthier, more sustainable farming systems.

- Promotion of Biodiversity: Garlic can attract beneficial insects that help control pests, contributing to a healthier and more diverse ecosystem on the farm.

- Soil Health Improvement: Garlic farming helps improve soil structure, adds organic matter, and enhances microbial activity. This benefits not only the garlic crop but also subsequent crops in the rotation.

4. Culinary and Cultural Significance

Garlic holds significant culinary and cultural importance worldwide. It is a staple ingredient in many traditional cuisines, adding its distinct flavour and aroma to various dishes. The cultural significance of garlic has helped in preserving its legacy, ensuring a sustained demand and market for garlic.

1.3 Market Demand for Garlic

Garlic has experienced a significant surge in market demand in recent years, making it a highly sought-after crop in the agricultural industry. This increased demand stems from various factors, including its unique flavour, versatile culinary uses, potential health benefits, and cultural significance. Let's delve into the market demand for garlic and the factors driving its popularity:

1. Growing Culinary Appreciation

Garlic is a fundamental ingredient in numerous culinary traditions worldwide. Its distinct flavour and aroma enhance the taste of a wide range of dishes, making it a staple in various cuisines. Garlic's versatility allows it to be used in soups, sauces, marinades, stir-fries, and countless other dishes. As global culinary trends continue to evolve, the demand for garlic remains strong, ensuring a consistent market for this versatile crop.

2. Health and Wellness Trends

The increasing awareness of the potential health benefits of garlic has contributed to its growing demand. Garlic is rich in vital nutrients and bioactive compounds that have been linked to various health advantages. As people become more health-conscious, the demand for functional foods, such as garlic, has increased. Consumers are looking for natural ingredients that can offer nutritional support and potential disease prevention. Garlic's reputation for promoting cardiovascular health, supporting the immune system, and potentially reducing the risk of certain types of cancer has further fueled its demand.

3. Cultural Significance and Tradition

Garlic holds cultural significance in many regions across the globe. It has been used in traditional medicine, religious rituals, and culinary traditions for centuries. The cultural importance given to garlic has helped perpetuate its demand, even in the face of increasing competition from other crops. Festivals and events celebrating garlic have gained popularity, attracting both locals and tourists. These events serve as a platform to promote the value and unique characteristics of garlic, supporting its demand and market growth.

4. Global Trade and Consumption

The global market for garlic has seen remarkable expansion in recent years. As international trade continues to thrive, the demand for garlic has increased, both for domestic consumption and export purposes. Countries like China, India, Spain, the United States, and South Korea are significant contributors to the global garlic market. The rise of e-commerce platforms has made it easier for consumers to access garlic products from around the world, further stimulating its demand.

5. Culinary and Food Service Industries

The culinary and food service industries play a vital role in driving the market demand for garlic. Restaurants, cafes, and catering businesses consistently incorporate garlic into their menus, using it as a flavor enhancer and key ingredient. As these industries grow and evolve, the demand for garlic as a culinary essential continues to rise. Additionally, the increasing popularity of ready-to-use, pre-peeled or chopped garlic products has expanded garlic's reach to a wider consumer base.

Chapter Two

Getting Started with Garlic Farming

2.1 Selecting the Right Garlic Varieties

Selecting the right garlic varieties is crucial when starting a garlic farming venture. Different garlic varieties have unique characteristics, growth requirements, and flavour profiles. Choosing the right garlic varieties can greatly impact the success and profitability of your garlic farming operation. Here are some key factors to consider when selecting garlic varieties for your farm:

1. Adaptability to Local Climate and Soil Conditions
One of the most important considerations when choosing garlic varieties is their adaptability to the local climate and soil conditions. Garlic varieties vary in their tolerance to

different climates, such as cold winters or hot summers. It is essential to select varieties that can thrive in your specific region's climate, ensuring optimal growth and yield. Additionally, certain garlic varieties may have specific soil preferences, such as well-drained soil or loamy soil. Assessing your farm's climate and soil conditions will help you narrow down the garlic varieties that are most suitable for your location.

2. Bulb Size and Yield Potential

The size of the garlic bulbs and their yield potential are essential considerations for garlic farmers. Different garlic varieties can produce bulbs of varying sizes, ranging from small to large. Consider market demand and your target customers when selecting garlic varieties based on bulb size. Additionally, pay attention to the yield potential of the garlic varieties. Some garlic varieties may be known for their high yields, while others may be smaller but have unique flavor profiles that appeal to niche markets. Balancing bulb size and yield potential will help you choose garlic varieties that align with your farm's goals and market requirements.

3. Flavor and Culinary Characteristics

Flavour is a crucial factor to consider when selecting garlic varieties, especially if you plan to cater to the culinary market. Different garlic varieties exhibit unique flavour profiles, ranging from mild and sweet to bold and pungent. Understanding the flavour characteristics of garlic varieties will enable you to select varieties that cater to specific culinary preferences and local taste preferences. Some varieties are more suitable for raw consumption in salads and dressings, while others are ideal for cooking and flavouring various dishes. Consider the end-use of your garlic and choose varieties that align with the culinary profiles desired by your target market.

4. Disease Resistance

Garlic is susceptible to various diseases and pests that can significantly impact crop yield and quality. When selecting garlic varieties, it is essential to consider their disease resistance traits. Some garlic varieties may be more resistant to common diseases such as white rot or garlic rust. By choosing disease-resistant varieties, you can reduce the risk of crop loss and decrease the need for chemical interventions. Research and consult with local agricultural extension services or experienced garlic farmers to identify garlic varieties that have a reputation for disease resistance in your region.

5. Availability and Market Demand

Availability and market demand play a crucial role in selecting garlic varieties for your farm. Some garlic varieties may be more readily available in your region, making it easier to access seed garlic bulbs for planting. Additionally, consider the market demand for specific garlic varieties. Research the preferences and trends in your target market to identify varieties that are in high demand. This will ensure a ready market for your garlic and potentially increase your profitability.

2.2 Preparing the Farm Land for Garlic Cultivation

Preparing the farmland is a crucial step in garlic farming that sets the foundation for successful cultivation. Proper land preparation ensures optimal growing conditions for garlic, promotes healthy plant growth, and maximizes yield. Here are some essential steps to follow when preparing the farmland for garlic cultivation:

1. Soil Testing and Analysis

Before starting any farmland preparation, it is essential to conduct a comprehensive soil test and analysis. Soil testing provides vital information about the soil's nutrient content, pH level, organic matter, and texture. Understanding the characteristics of your soil will help you make informed decisions regarding soil amendments and nutrient management. Soil testing also helps identify any potential deficiencies or imbalances that could affect garlic growth. Based on the soil test results, you can adjust the soil's pH levels and incorporate appropriate organic matter or fertilizers to create optimal growing conditions for garlic.

2. Clearing and Leveling the Land

Once you have obtained soil test results, the next step is to clear and level the land. Remove any existing vegetation, rocks, or debris from the field to create a clean growing space for garlic. Clearing the land also involves addressing any drainage issues. Ensure proper water flow by leveling the field and addressing any slopes or trenches that may impede drainage. Proper land leveling prevents waterlogging, which can lead to root rot and other fungal diseases.

3. Organic Matter Incorporation

Incorporating organic matter into the soil is crucial for enhancing soil fertility, drainage, and moisture-retention capacity. Organic matter such as compost, well-rotted manure, or cover crops can be incorporated into the soil during land preparation. Organic matter improves soil structure, promotes microbial activity, and increases nutrient availability. Spread a layer of compost or well-rotted manure over the field and incorporate it into the soil using plows or tillers. This process helps replenish soil nutrients and enhances the soil's organic content, ensuring a fertile environment for garlic growth.

4. Soil Amendments and Fertilizer Application

Based on the soil test results, you may need to apply specific soil amendments and fertilizers to address any nutrient deficiencies or imbalances. Certain garlic varieties have specific nutrient requirements, so it is essential to ensure that the soil provides the necessary nutrients for healthy plant growth. Incorporate recommended fertilizers or organic amendments, such as bone meal, rock phosphate, or blood meal, into the soil during land preparation. Follow the recommended application rates and methods to ensure proper distribution of nutrients throughout the growing area.

5. Bed Preparation

Preparing raised beds or ridges is a common practice in garlic farming. Raised beds offer improved drainage, prevent waterlogging, and create a suitable environment for garlic bulb development. Using a tractor or farm implements, create raised beds or ridges that are approximately 8 to 12 inches high and 36 to 42 inches wide. Space the beds about 30 to 36 inches apart to provide sufficient room for garlic plants to grow and facilitate efficient tractor or equipment access for subsequent farm operations.

6. Irrigation System Installation

Installing an efficient irrigation system is essential for maintaining adequate moisture levels during garlic cultivation. Garlic requires consistent moisture throughout its growing cycle, particularly during bulb development. Depending on the scale of your garlic farming operation, choose an irrigation system that suits your needs, such as drip irrigation, overhead sprinklers, or furrow irrigation. Proper irrigation ensures optimal garlic plant growth, helps prevent diseases, and promotes bulb development.

7. Weed Control and Mulching

To suppress weed growth and conserve soil moisture, consider implementing mulching practices. After planting the garlic cloves, apply a layer of organic mulch, such as straw or hay, over the beds. Mulch helps inhibit weed growth, retains soil moisture, regulates soil temperature, and enhances overall crop yield. Regularly monitor the field for weed growth and take appropriate measures, such as manual weeding or using herbicides, to keep the garlic beds weed-free.

2.3 Soil Testing and Soil Preparation

Soil testing and preparation are fundamental steps when starting a garlic farming venture. Understanding the characteristics of your soil and ensuring its optimal condition are crucial for successful garlic cultivation. By conducting soil tests and implementing proper soil preparation techniques, you can create a fertile environment that supports healthy garlic growth and maximizes your crop yield. Here's a comprehensive guide on soil testing and soil preparation for garlic farming:

1. Soil Testing: Assessing Soil Health

Soil testing is the first step in determining the health and fertility of your soil. It provides valuable information about the nutrient content, pH level, organic matter, and texture of the soil. Soil tests help identify any deficiencies or imbalances that may affect garlic growth and guide you in making informed decisions regarding soil amendments and nutrient management. To conduct a soil test, collect soil samples from various areas of your field using a soil probe or auger. Ensure that the samples are representative of the entire field by collecting samples at different depths and locations. Send the soil samples to a reputable soil testing laboratory for analysis.

2. Interpreting Soil Test Results

Once you receive the soil test results, it is crucial to interpret the data accurately. The soil test report will provide information about the nutrient levels in your soil, soil pH, and any specific recommendations for amendments or adjustments. Pay attention to the nutrient levels and assess if any essential nutrients are deficient or excessive. Consider the recommended pH range for garlic cultivation, which is typically between 6.0 and 7.5. If the soil pH is outside this range, appropriate measures may be needed to adjust it. Use the soil test report as a guide to understand your soil's requirements and tailor your soil preparation accordingly.

3. Soil Amendments: Correcting Imbalances

Based on the soil test results, you may need to apply specific soil amendments to correct nutrient deficiencies or imbalances. Garlic has specific nutrient requirements, particularly for sulfur, phosphorus, and potassium. Adequate levels of these nutrients are crucial for garlic bulb development and overall plant health. Depending on your soil test results and the specific nutrient requirements, you may need to incorporate organic amendments or apply mineral fertilizers to correct any imbalances. Common amendments include organic matter, such as compost or well-rotted manure, which increase soil fertility and improve its structure. Additionally, you may need to add specific mineral fertilizers based on the nutrient requirements identified in the soil test report.

4. Organic Matter Incorporation: Enhancing Soil Fertility

Incorporating organic matter into the soil is essential for enhancing soil fertility and promoting healthy garlic growth. Organic matter, such as compost or well-rotted manure, improves soil structure, enhances moisture retention, stimulates microbial activity, and increases nutrient availability. Spread a layer of organic matter over the field during soil preparation and incorporate it into the soil using plows or tillers. This process helps improve soil texture, nutrient content, and overall soil health, providing an ideal environment for garlic root development and bulb formation.

5. Tillage and Soil Structure

Proper tillage practices play a crucial role in soil preparation for garlic farming. Tillage helps break up compacted soil, improve aeration, and facilitate root penetration. However, it is important to strike a balance, as excessive tillage can disrupt soil structure and lead to erosion. Depending on your soil conditions, use appropriate tillage equipment to loosen the soil and create a fine seedbed. Avoid working the soil when it is excessively moist, as it can lead to compaction and damage the soil structure. Regularly monitor soil moisture levels and adjust your tillage practices accordingly to maintain optimal soil structure for garlic cultivation.

6. Bed Formation: Raised Beds or Ridging

Creating raised beds or ridges is a common practice in garlic farming. Raised beds offer improved drainage, prevent waterlogging, and promote healthy root development. Using a tractor or farm implements, form raised beds or ridges that are approximately 8 to 12 inches high and 36 to 42 inches wide. The spacing between beds should be about 30 to 36 inches to allow sufficient room for garlic plants to grow and facilitate efficient tractor or equipment access for subsequent farm operations. Proper bed formation enhances soil drainage, prevents waterlogged conditions, and promotes optimal garlic growth.

7. Mulching: Weed Control and Moisture Retention

Mulching is an effective practice for suppressing weed growth, conserving soil moisture, and maintaining optimal soil temperature for garlic cultivation. After planting the garlic cloves, apply a layer of organic mulch, such as straw or hay, over the beds. Mulch helps inhibit weed germination and growth, reduces water evaporation from the soil surface, moderates soil temperature fluctuations, and improves overall crop yield. Regularly monitor the mulch layer and replenish it as needed throughout the growing season to ensure consistent weed suppression and moisture retention.

2.4 Climate and Environmental Considerations

Garlic farming is a versatile agricultural activity that can be practiced in various climate conditions and environmental settings. However, the success of garlic cultivation relies heavily on the appropriate selection of garlic varieties and suitable environmental conditions such as temperature, moisture, and soil conditions. When starting a garlic farming venture, it's crucial to consider the critical climate and environmental factors that affect garlic growth and yield. Here's a comprehensive guide to climate and environmental considerations when getting started with garlic farming:

1. Temperature Requirements:

Garlic is a cool-season crop that thrives in moderate temperatures. Garlic plants have specific temperature requirements for optimal growth, bulb development, and yield. The ideal temperature range for growing garlic is between 12°C to 24°C (54°F to 75°F) during the growing season. Exposure to extreme temperature variations, either hot or cold, can negatively impact garlic growth and development. Extremely cold weather can prevent proper bulb formation, while high temperatures above 30°C (86°F) during bulb formation can reduce bulb size and quality. Choose garlic varieties that are adapted to your region's temperature conditions and modify your planting schedule according to the anticipated temperature ranges.

2. Moisture Requirements:

Garlic requires consistent moisture throughout its growing cycle for optimal growth and bulb development. Adequate soil moisture levels ensure that the plant roots have sufficient water to take up essential nutrients. However, excess moisture or waterlogging can lead to root rot and other fungal diseases. To ensure optimal moisture conditions, consider the local rainfall patterns, soil drainage, and irrigation systems. Depending on the weather patterns, you may need to adjust your watering schedule or use suitable irrigation equipment like drip, overhead sprinklers, or furrow irrigation systems. Proper water management is necessary to maximize garlic yield and quality.

3. Soil Type and Nutrient Availability:

Soil type and nutrient availability are crucial factors that affect garlic growth and development. Garlic prefers loamy soil types that are well-draining and rich in organic matter. Adequate soil preparation through the incorporation of organic matter, soil amendments, and other appropriate techniques can enhance soil quality and promote optimal garlic growth. To ensure sufficient nutrient availability, soil testing and analysis are essential. Soil tests help identify any deficiencies or imbalances in the soil nutrient content, enabling the application of specific fertilizers or organic matter to address these needs.

4. Environmental Factors:

Environmental factors such as wind, sunlight, and air circulation have a significant impact on garlic growth and survival. Garlic plants exposed to high winds are susceptible to dehydration and windburn. They require a sheltered growing environment to minimize wind damage and maximize yield. Apart from wind, garlic also requires sufficient exposure to sunlight to facilitate photosynthesis, carbohydrate accumulation, and optimal bulb growth. Garlic plants that grow under shady or insufficiently lit conditions develop weak and unhealthy foliage, resulting in reduced bulb size and crop yield. Proper air circulation is also critical for garlic farming. Proper spacing between garlic plants and the creation of raised beds or ridges can promote air circulation that discourages fungal and bacterial diseases.

5. Pest and Disease Management:

Pest and disease management are essential aspects of garlic farming, given that garlic is susceptible to pests such as onion maggots, thrips, and root nematodes. Garlic is also prone to fungal diseases such as white rot, purple blotch, and basal rot. To mitigate the risk of these pests and diseases, consider implementing suitable pest management practices, such as crop rotation, use of disease-resistant garlic varieties, and preventive measures. Incorporating organic matter, maintaining optimal soil moisture levels, and good air circulation can also reduce the risk of fungal diseases.

Chapter Three

Planting and Growing Garlic

3.1 Choosing the Right Planting Method

Choosing the right planting method is essential for successful garlic farming. The planting method you select will impact garlic growth, bulb formation, weed control, and overall crop yield. Various techniques can be used for planting and growing garlic, each with its advantages and considerations. When deciding on the planting method, factors such as soil type, available resources, garlic variety, and farming practices should be taken into account. Here are some common planting methods for garlic and their key considerations:

1. Direct Seeding:

Direct seeding is a simple and cost-effective method for planting garlic. In this method, garlic cloves are sown directly into the soil where they will grow. Direct seeding works best in areas with mild climates and loamy, well-draining soils. Before planting, prepare the soil by incorporating organic matter and ensuring good soil fertility. Divide the garlic bulb into individual cloves and plant them with the pointed end up, spacing them about 4 to 6 inches apart in rows. Cover the cloves with soil, ensuring they are planted at a depth of about 2 inches. The main advantage of direct seeding is that it requires less labour and allows for natural development and establishment of garlic plants. However, it may be more challenging to control weeds and pests compared to other planting methods.

2. Transplanting:

Transplanting is a popular planting method for garlic, especially in regions with shorter growing seasons or colder climates. In this method, garlic cloves are first planted in trays or pots indoors or in a protected environment, such as a greenhouse or a cold frame. This allows the garlic to germinate and establish roots before being transplanted into the field. Transplanting allows for an early start to the growing season and provides better control over garlic spacing, weed management, and establishment. Once the weather and soil conditions are suitable, carefully transplant the garlic seedlings into prepared beds or ridges in the field. The advantages of transplanting include better weed control and the ability to optimize planting dates for improved garlic growth and yield. However, transplanting requires additional time, effort, and resources for seedling production.

3. Raised Beds or Ridging:

Raised beds or ridging is a planting method commonly used in garlic farming. This method involves creating elevated rows or ridges that provide improved soil drainage, better moisture retention, and enhanced root development. Use a tractor or suitable farm equipment to form rows or ridges approximately 8 to 12 inches high and 36 to 42 inches wide. The spacing between beds should be about 30 to 36 inches to allow sufficient room for garlic plants to grow and facilitate efficient tractor or equipment access for subsequent farm operations. Plant the garlic cloves in the furrows or depressions of the raised beds and cover them with soil, ensuring the cloves are planted at the recommended depth. Raised beds or ridging help prevent waterlogging, improve soil aeration, and facilitate weed control. This method is particularly beneficial in areas with heavy or poorly drained soils.

4. Intercropping:

Intercropping refers to the practice of growing garlic alongside other crops in the same field. This planting method maximizes land utilization and can provide added benefits such as pest control, weed suppression, and improved overall farm productivity. When intercropping garlic, ensure that the companion crops are compatible with garlic's growth requirements and do not compete for resources. Select companion crops that have a compatible growth habit, mature at different times, and are known to have positive interactions with garlic.

3.2 Timing and Properly Spacing Garlic Bulbs

Timing and proper spacing are crucial factors for successful garlic farming. The timing of planting garlic bulbs and the spacing between them can significantly impact garlic growth, bulb size, and overall yield. Properly spacing the garlic bulbs allows each plant to have sufficient access to nutrients, water, and sunlight, promoting healthy development. Additionally, timing the planting of garlic bulbs ensures that they have optimal conditions for growth and establishment. Here is a comprehensive guide to timing and properly spacing garlic bulbs for planting and growing garlic:

1. Timing of Garlic Planting:

The timing of garlic planting is essential for achieving optimal growth and maximizing bulb development. Garlic plants have specific growth requirements that vary based on the garlic variety and local climate. In general, garlic planting is done in the fall or early winter, allowing the bulbs to establish roots before entering a period of dormancy during winter. The exact planting time depends on the climate and temperature conditions in your region. Ideally, garlic should be planted about 4 to 6 weeks before the ground freezes. This allows the roots to develop and plants to establish themselves before winter sets in. In milder climates, where the ground doesn't freeze, garlic can be planted in late autumn. By planting at the right time, you provide the bulbs with favourable conditions for growth and ensure they have sufficient time to develop before the onset of warmer weather in spring.

2. Spacing Garlic Bulbs:

Properly spacing garlic bulbs is crucial to allow each plant to receive adequate sunlight, water, and nutrients for optimal growth and bulb development. The spacing requirements vary depending on the garlic variety, bulb size, and planting method. A general guideline is to space the garlic bulbs about 4 to 6 inches apart in rows. This spacing allows enough room for the plants to grow and prevents overcrowding, which can result in competition for resources, increased disease incidence, and smaller bulb sizes. For raised beds or ridging planting methods, space the rows approximately 30 to 36 inches apart. This wider spacing between rows enables efficient farm operations and provides ample space for the garlic plants to expand. It's important to maintain consistent spacing throughout the garlic field to ensure uniform growth and optimal utilization of resources.

3. Adjusting Spacing for Seed Size and Planting Method:
The spacing requirements can be adjusted based on the size of the garlic cloves and the planting method used. Larger cloves generally produce larger bulbs, while smaller cloves yield smaller bulbs. If you have larger garlic bulbs with bigger cloves, you may opt for slightly wider spacing to allow more room for bulb expansion. Conversely, smaller cloves may be planted slightly closer together to maximize space utilization. Additionally, the choice of planting method may influence spacing considerations. For example, if you are using the raised bed or ridging method,

wider spacing between rows may be preferred to accommodate equipment access and facilitate efficient farm operations. However, if you are using direct seeding or intercropping methods, closer spacing between plants may be required to optimize land utilization and maximize yield.

4. Weed Control and Air Circulation:

Proper spacing of garlic bulbs also plays a role in weed control and air circulation. Adequate spacing allows for easy access to remove weeds manually and reduces the competition for nutrients and water. It also promotes better air circulation between plants, which helps prevent the buildup of moisture and reduces the risk of fungal diseases. Good air circulation ensures that the leaves dry quickly after rainfall or irrigation, minimizing the conditions favorable for fungal growth. Avoid overcrowding the garlic plants, as it can create a favourable environment for pests and diseases and lead to poor bulb formation.

5. Crop Rotation and Succession Planting:

In addition to proper spacing, crop rotation and succession planting are important considerations for garlic farming. Avoid planting garlic in the same area or following closely related crops (such as onions and leeks) to reduce the risk of disease build-up in the soil. Introducing a rotation cycle of at least three years can help break pest and disease cycles and maintain soil health. Succession planting, which involves planting garlic in batches or at regular intervals, allows for a continuous harvest throughout the season, maximizing yield and extending the availability of fresh garlic.

3.3 Planting Techniques: Beds, Rows, and Raised Beds

Planting techniques play a critical role in the success of garlic farming. The planting method you choose can have a significant impact on garlic growth, development, pest management, and overall yield. The most common planting techniques for garlic include planting in beds, rows, and raised beds. Each technique has its advantages, disadvantages, and specific considerations. In this guide, we'll explore the benefits and challenges of each technique and provide guidance on how to choose the best method for your garlic farming operation.

1. Planting Garlic in Beds:

Planting garlic in beds is one of the most common techniques for garlic farming. A bed is typically a raised, narrowed strip of soil that allows for efficient irrigation and drainage. When planting garlic in beds, space the garlic cloves about 4-6 inches apart and around 2 inches deep. Rows should be spaced about 6 inches apart. The advantages of planting garlic in beds include:

- Better drainage: Planting garlic in beds provides better drainage than planting in straight rows. The raised bed allows water to drain away more effectively, reducing the risk of waterlogging.

- Improved soil aeration: Planting garlic in beds allows for better soil aeration, allowing oxygen to reach the roots more efficiently. This can help prevent root rot and other diseases.

- Improved root development: The garlic roots have more room to grow in a bed, allowing for better absorption of nutrients, water, and oxygen.

- One disadvantage of planting garlic in beds is that it can require more resources in terms of soil preparation and maintenance. It may also be challenging to manage weeds and pests in the narrow growing areas.

2. Planting Garlic in Rows:

Planting garlic in rows is another common method used in garlic farming. This involves tilling the soil into straight furrows (trenches) and planting the garlic cloves in the furrows. The cloves should be placed about 4-6 inches apart, and the rows should be spaced about 18-24 inches apart. The advantages of planting garlic in rows include:

- Efficient use of space: Planting garlic in rows allows for efficient use of space, making it easier to manage the crop and harvest.
- Straightforward planting: Planting garlic in rows is a simple planting method that requires minimal labor and resources.

- Easy to manage weeds and pests: Planting garlic in rows allows for efficient weed and pest management.

- A disadvantage of planting garlic in rows is that it may result in poor drainage and soil compaction in walkways. This can lead to waterlogging, reduced oxygen, and nutrient availability, and increased pest problems.

3. Planting Garlic in Raised Beds:

Planting garlic in raised beds involves creating elevated beds or ridges that provide improved soil drainage and moisture retention. In this method, use a tractor or suitable farm equipment to form ridges that are approximately 8 to 12 inches high and 36-42 inches wide. The garlic bulbs are then planted in the furrows or depressions of the raised beds, with approximately 6 inches between each bulb and

30-36 inches between rows. The advantages of planting garlic in raised beds include:

- Improved soil drainage: Raised beds provide improved soil drainage and prevent waterlogging, making it easier to manage the moisture levels of the garlic.
- Reduced soil compaction: Raised beds can help prevent soil compaction, preserving soil structure and promoting optimal root development.
- Improved weed management: The narrow growing area of the raised bed makes it easier to manage weeds manually or mechanically.

3.4 Irrigation and Watering Practices for Garlic

Garlic requires enough water to grow and develop properly. Insufficient water can lead to stunted growth, reduced yield, and poor bulb formation, while excess moisture can cause root rot, mould, and other diseases. Irrigation and watering practices are, therefore, crucial factors in the overall success of garlic farming. In this guide, we'll explore the best irrigation and watering practices for planting and growing garlic.

1. Soil Composition and Watering Frequency:

The soil type and structure play a significant role in determining the watering frequency for garlic farming. Sandy soils drain faster and require more frequent watering than soils with a high clay content. Before planting garlic, the soil must be prepared to ensure optimal water utilization and drainage. The bed or planting area should be well-drained to prevent waterlogging and promote optimal root development. Ensure that the soil is well-draining, with good air circulation and water-holding capacity. To determine if the soil is too dry and requires watering, use the finger test. Stick your finger in the soil up to the first knuckle. If the soil feels dry, then it's time to water.

2. Timing of Irrigation:

The timing of watering is crucial when it comes to garlic farming. Water the soil immediately after planting the garlic to provide sufficient moisture for establishing roots. However, it's essential to avoid overwatering during the first few weeks after planting to prevent rotting of the cloves. Once the garlic has established, it's best to water regularly to maintain the right moisture levels. Avoid watering when it's too sunny since this results in rapid evaporation. Watering in the morning or evening helps prevent water loss due to evaporation and allows for proper water absorption by the garlic roots.

3. Drip Irrigation:

Drip irrigation is an effective method for providing water for garlic farming. It involves providing water directly to the base of the plants via tubing with small holes running along its length. The tubing is placed above or below the soil surface for efficient and controlled water delivery. Drip irrigation ensures that the moisture goes straight to the roots, providing them with sufficient water without wastage or oversaturation. Drip irrigation also minimizes soil compaction and maintains soil temperature and moisture levels.

4. Mulching:

Mulching is the practice of covering the soil surface around the garlic plants with organic materials, such as straw, leaves, or grass clippings. Mulching helps to conserve soil moisture by reducing water evaporation from the soil surface. Additionally, it helps in weed suppression and maintaining soil temperature. It also serves as insulation and protects the garlic roots from sudden and extreme temperature changes.

5. Overwatering:

Overwatering is a common challenge with garlic farming. Overwatering leads to soil saturation, which leads to poor garlic growth, fungus, and root rot. Excess moisture can also encourage the growth of pests such as slugs and snails. It's important not to over-water the plants and instead opt for a gradual and regular watering schedule. Avoid watering too much during the dormant period, which can result in bulb cracking and rotting when it's time to harvest.

Chapter Four

Managing Soil Nutrients and Fertilisers

4.1 Soil Fertility and Nutrient Requirements for Garlic

Maintaining soil fertility and providing the right nutrients is essential for the healthy growth and development of garlic plants. Garlic requires a well-balanced supply of nutrients to produce robust foliage, large bulbs, and high yields. Understanding the nutrient requirements of garlic and implementing appropriate soil management practices can significantly impact the success of garlic farming. In this guide, we'll explore the importance of soil fertility, the nutrient requirements of garlic, and best practices for managing soil nutrients and fertilizers.

1. Importance of Soil Fertility:

Soil fertility refers to the soil's capacity to provide essential nutrients and support healthy plant growth. Maintaining soil fertility is crucial for garlic farming, as nutrient deficiency or imbalance can lead to stunted growth, reduced bulb size, and lower yields. Fertile soil promotes the development of strong garlic plants with robust root systems, enabling efficient nutrient uptake and utilisation. Additionally, fertile soil helps protect against diseases and pests, enhances plant resistance to environmental stresses, and improves soil structure and water-holding capacity.

2. Nutrient Requirements of Garlic:

The nutrient requirements of garlic can vary based on factors such as soil type, garlic variety, climate, and farming practices. However, some essential nutrients are vital for healthy garlic growth, including:

- Nitrogen (N): Nitrogen is crucial for promoting leaf growth and overall plant vigor. Garlic requires a steady supply of nitrogen throughout its growth stages, with higher amounts needed during vegetative growth. Organic sources, such as composted manure or nitrogen-rich fertilizers, can help meet the nitrogen requirements of garlic.

- Phosphorus (P): Phosphorus is important for root development, flower formation, and bulb growth. Adequate phosphorus helps ensure the production of large, well-formed garlic bulbs. Phosphorus can be supplied through organic sources like bone meal or rock phosphate.

- Potassium (K): Potassium plays a significant role in garlic's overall health and disease resistance. It enhances the plant's ability to withstand drought, pests, and diseases. Potassium can be provided through organic sources such as wood ash or potassium sulfate.

- Micronutrients: Garlic also requires micronutrients, such as iron, manganese, zinc, and copper, albeit in smaller quantities. These micronutrients play crucial roles in various plant processes and can be supplied through commercial micronutrient fertilizers or organic amendments.

3. Soil Testing and Fertilization:

To manage soil nutrients effectively, it's essential to conduct regular soil testing to assess nutrient levels and pH. Soil testing provides vital information on the nutrient status and pH of the soil, allowing for targeted fertilizer application. By knowing the soil nutrient levels, farmers can make informed decisions about the types and amounts of fertilizers to apply.

Based on soil test results, organic or conventional fertilizers can be used to supplement the nutrient requirements of garlic. Organic fertilizers, such as compost, well-rotted manure, or bone meal, not only supply essential nutrients but also improve soil structure and microbial activity. Conventional fertilizers, such as granular or liquid fertilizers, can be used to provide specific nutrient ratios and meet the plant's immediate needs.

It's important to follow the recommended application rates and timing guidelines when applying fertilizers. Over-fertilization can result in nutrient imbalances, leaching, or environmental pollution, while under-fertilization can lead to nutrient deficiencies and reduced yields. Split applications during different growth stages of garlic can help ensure a continuous supply of nutrients.

4. Crop Rotation and Cover Crops:

Crop rotation and the use of cover crops are effective practices for managing soil fertility and nutrient requirements in garlic farming. Rotating crops helps break pest and disease cycles, prevents nutrient depletion, and promotes overall soil health. The inclusion of leguminous cover crops, such as clover or vetch, can help fix atmospheric nitrogen, improving soil nitrogen levels for subsequent garlic crops.

5. Organic Matter and Soil Amendments:

Adding organic matter, such as compost or well-rotted manure, is beneficial for maintaining soil fertility. Organic matter improves soil structure, enhances water retention, and supplies essential nutrients as it decomposes. Additionally, the incorporation of soil amendments, such as lime to adjust pH levels or gypsum to improve soil drainage, can contribute to optimal soil fertility for garlic growth.

4.2 Organic and Inorganic Fertilizers for Garlic Farming

Garlic is a nutrient-dense crop that requires adequate nutrition for optimal growth and yield. Soil fertility plays a vital role in providing the essential nutrients for garlic plants. Fertilizers are an essential component of soil fertility management, and there are two main categories of fertilizers: organic and inorganic. In this guide, we'll explore the differences between organic and inorganic fertilizers, their advantages and disadvantages, and their suitability for garlic farming.

Organic Fertilizers for Garlic Farming:

Organic fertilizers are derived from natural sources, such as compost, manure, bone meal, or fish emulsion. These fertilizers are considered to be more sustainable and environmentally friendly because they are derived from renewable resources without the use of synthetic chemicals.

Organic fertilizers provide several benefits for garlic farming. Firstly, they supply the essential plant nutrients, such as nitrogen, phosphorus, and potassium, in a slow-release form, minimizing the risk of nutrient leaching and promoting long-term soil health. Secondly, organic fertilizers improve soil structure, enhance water-holding capacity and microbial activity, and contribute to soil organic matter accumulation. Thirdly, organic fertilizers reduce the risk of chemical buildup in the soil, protecting plant and human health.

However, organic fertilizers have some limitations. They may contain lower nutrient concentrations than synthetic fertilizers, requiring larger application rates. Also, due to their slow-release nature, they may take longer to see the desired results. Finally, organic fertilizers may be contaminated with weed seeds, pathogens, or heavy metals that may negatively impact crop growth.

Some common organic fertilizers used for garlic farming include:

- Compost: Compost is an excellent source of organic matter and essential plant nutrients. It improves soil fertility and structure, provides slow-release nutrients, and enhances microbial activity.

- Manure: Manure is another rich source of organic matter and nutrients. It is commonly used as a soil amendment for garlic farming, providing slow-release nutrients that enhance soil fertility and microbial activity.

- Fish emulsion: Fish emulsion is an organic fertilizer made from ground fish waste. It is a concentrated source of nitrogen, phosphorus, and potassium, providing a quick nutrient boost for garlic growth.

Inorganic Fertilizers for Garlic Farming:

Inorganic or synthetic fertilizers are manufactured through chemical processes, providing nutrients in concentrated forms that are highly accessible to plants. Inorganic fertilizers are often used in commercial agriculture due to their affordability, ease of use, and quick results.

Inorganic fertilizers provide several benefits for garlic farming. Firstly, they are highly concentrated and rapidly release nutrients for optimal plant growth. Secondly, they offer precise nutrient control, enabling farmers to tailor fertilizer applications to specific plant needs. Thirdly, inorganic fertilizers can be used in conjunction with soil testing and nutrient management plans to optimize fertilizer use, minimizing waste and environmental impacts.

However, inorganic fertilizers also have some drawbacks. They may contain high concentrations of salts and other chemicals that can damage plant roots or buildup in the soil over time. The overuse or misuse of inorganic fertilizers can lead to environmental pollution, nutrient runoff, and negative impacts on soil fertility. Finally, inorganic fertilizers do not provide the same benefits to soil structure, microbial activity, or long-term soil health as organic fertilizers.

Some common inorganic fertilizers used for garlic farming include:

- Nitrogen fertilisers: Nitrogen fertilizers are essential for garlic growth and development. They are available in various forms, including ammonium nitrate, urea, and ammonium sulfate, providing a quick release of nitrogen to the plants.

- Phosphorus fertilizers: Phosphorus fertilizers are critical for root development, flower formation, and bulb growth. They are available in different forms such as mono-ammonium phosphate (MAP) or triple superphosphate (TSP).

- Potassium fertilizers: Potassium fertilizers play a vital role in garlic's overall health, disease resistance, and stress tolerance. They are available in various forms such as potassium chloride or potassium sulfate.

Choosing the Right Fertilizer for Garlic Farming:

Choosing the right type of fertilizer for garlic farming depends on several factors. Soil type, nutrient status, and garlic variety are essential considerations. Soil testing is an essential tool to determine the fertilizer needs of the crop, enable nutrient management planning, and ensure optimal fertilizer use.

Organic fertilizers are generally best used to improve long-term soil fertility and sustainability, but they may require larger application rates and longer time to see the desired results. Inorganic fertilizers provide quick nutrient availability and precision nutrient control, but their overuse or misuse can lead to soil degradation and environmental issues.

4.3 Compost and Organic Matter Application

Compost and organic matter application play a significant role in managing soil nutrients and fertilizers in garlic farming. The use of organic amendments, such as compost, helps improve soil structure, enhance nutrient availability, and promote overall soil health. In this guide, we'll explore the benefits of compost and organic matter application, the process of making and applying compost, and how they contribute to successful garlic farming.

Benefits of Compost and Organic Matter Application for Garlic Farming:

Compost and organic matter applications offer several advantages for garlic farming:

- Nutrient Supply: Compost and organic matter are rich in essential plant nutrients, providing a slow-release source of nitrogen, phosphorus, potassium, and micronutrients. The gradual nutrient release ensures a continuous supply of nutrients, reducing the risk of nutrient deficiencies or excesses that can negatively impact garlic growth and yield.

- Soil Structure Improvement: Compost and organic matter enhance soil structure by improving aeration, water-holding capacity, and drainage. The increased soil porosity promotes root development, facilitates nutrient uptake, and reduces the risk of soil compaction, particularly in heavy clay soils.

- Microbial Activity Enhancement: Compost and organic matter serve as a food source for beneficial soil microorganisms, improving microbial activity, and diversity. These microorganisms play a crucial role in nutrient cycling, organic matter decomposition, and disease suppression. Healthy microbial populations contribute to overall soil health and support optimal garlic growth and productivity.

- Water Retention and Drought Tolerance: The addition of compost and organic matter improves the water-holding capacity of the soil, reducing water runoff and increasing water availability for plants. This benefit is particularly important in regions with erratic rainfall patterns or during dry periods, as it helps maintain soil moisture levels, supports plant water uptake, and enhances garlic's ability to withstand drought stress.

- Organic Matter Accumulation: Regular compost and organic matter application contribute to the long-term accumulation of organic matter in the soil. This organic matter serves as a reservoir for nutrients, enhances soil fertility, builds soil organic carbon, improves soil structure, and boosts overall soil health and sustainability.

Making and Applying Compost for Garlic Farming:

Making compost involves the decomposition of organic materials, such as plant residues, crop residues, animal manure, or kitchen scraps, into a nutrient-rich humus that can be used as a soil amendment. The process of making compost follows a few key steps:

- Material Selection: Choose a mix of carbon-rich (e.g., dry leaves, straw, wood chips) and nitrogen-rich (e.g., grass clippings, kitchen scraps, manure) materials. This balance of carbon and nitrogen ensures a proper breakdown of organic matter and the development of a stable compost.
- Composting Bin or Pile: Designate an area or use a composting bin to contain the compost materials. The composting pile should be well-aerated with the right moisture content (approximately 40-60% moisture).

- Layering and Mixing: Layer the compost materials, alternating between carbon-rich and nitrogen-rich materials. Mixing or turning the pile regularly promotes aeration, decomposition, and microbial activity.

- Time and Temperature: Composting typically takes several months to a year, depending on the materials used, pile size, and environmental conditions. The ideal temperature for composting is between 120-160°F (49-71°C), which supports efficient decomposition and kills weed seeds and pathogens.

- Curing and Application: Once the composting process is complete, allow the compost to cure for a few weeks to stabilize further. Then, it can be incorporated into the soil before planting garlic or applied as a top dressing during the growing season.

When applying compost to garlic fields, consider the following:

- Incorporate compost into the soil during land preparation or apply as a top dressing around garlic plants.

- Ensure a uniform distribution of compost to ensure even nutrient availability.

- Consider the compost's nutrient content and make adjustments to other fertilizer applications accordingly to avoid overapplication.

- Maintain appropriate soil moisture levels after compost application to support nutrient release and uptake.

Other Organic Matter Applications for Garlic Farming:

Apart from compost, other organic matter sources can be used to enhance soil fertility and manage soil nutrients in garlic farming. Some common organic matter sources include:

- Cover Crops: Planting cover crops, such as legumes, grasses, or mixtures, adds organic matter to the soil. Cover crops also improve nitrogen fixation, reduce weed pressure, and enhance soil structure when incorporated into the soil.

- Mulching: Mulching with organic materials, such as straw or hay, helps regulate soil temperature, control weed growth, conserve soil moisture, and add organic matter as it breaks down. Mulching also protects garlic bulbs from direct contact with the soil, reducing the risk of rot or fungal infections.

- Green Manure: Green manure crops, such as clover or vetch, can be grown specifically to be incorporated into the soil as green manure. These crops contribute nitrogen and organic matter, improve soil health, and enhance nutrient availability for subsequent garlic crops.

4.4 Foliar Feeding and Micronutrient Sprays

Foliar feeding and micronutrient sprays are valuable tools for managing soil nutrients and fertilizers in garlic farming. While soil amendments and fertilizers are essential for providing nutrients to the garlic plant, foliar feeding offers a complementary approach by providing nutrients directly to the leaves. In this guide, we will explore the benefits of foliar feeding, the role of micronutrient sprays, and best practices for incorporating these techniques into garlic farming.

Benefits of Foliar Feeding in Garlic Farming:

Foliar feeding, or the application of liquid nutrient solutions directly to the leaves, provides several advantages for garlic farming:

1. Rapid Nutrient Uptake: Foliar feeding allows for the quick absorption of nutrients by the garlic plant. The nutrients bypass the soil and root system, entering the plant through the stomata on the leaves. This efficient nutrient uptake can help address nutrient deficiencies promptly and provide a boost to the plant's growth and development.

2. Correcting Nutrient Imbalances: Foliar feeding is an effective way to correct nutrient imbalances in garlic plants. It allows specific nutrients, such as nitrogen, phosphorus, potassium, and secondary nutrients like calcium, magnesium, and sulfur, to be targeted and applied directly to the foliage. This targeted

approach helps address deficiencies and promotes healthy crop growth.

3. Overcoming Soil Limitations: In some cases, the soil may have nutrient limitations or imbalances that are challenging to correct through traditional soil amendment methods. Foliar feeding allows growers to bypass the limitations of the soil and directly supply the necessary nutrients to the plants. It provides a supplemental source of nutrients to support optimal garlic growth, especially in situations where the soil conditions are less than ideal.

4. Increased Nutrient Use Efficiency: Foliar feeding enhances nutrient use efficiency in garlic farming. Unlike soil-applied nutrients, which can be subject to leaching or immobilization, foliar-applied nutrients are readily available to the plant without the risk of loss. This targeted delivery reduces the

potential for nutrient wastage and ensures that the garlic plants receive the nutrients they need in a timely manner.

Role of Micronutrient Sprays in Garlic Farming:

Micronutrients are essential for healthy plant growth, even though they are required in smaller quantities compared to macronutrients. Micronutrient sprays are foliar applications specifically designed to address deficiencies in these essential trace elements, which include zinc, iron, manganese, copper, boron, and molybdenum. Here's the role micronutrient sprays play in garlic farming:

1. Micronutrient Correction: Garlic plants can sometimes experience deficiencies in specific micronutrients due to factors such as soil pH, soil nutrient availability, or plant uptake limitations. Micronutrient sprays provide a targeted approach to

supply these deficient trace elements directly to the plant, effectively correcting any imbalances and promoting healthy plant growth.

2. Improved Plant Health: Micronutrients play a crucial role in various physiological processes within the garlic plant. For example, iron is essential for chlorophyll synthesis, zinc is necessary for enzyme activation, and manganese is involved in photosynthesis. By applying micronutrient sprays, growers ensure that the garlic plants have access to these essential nutrients, promoting overall plant health and vigor.

3. Enhanced Pesticide Efficiency: Micronutrient sprays can act as adjuvants, improving the effectiveness of pesticides and fungicides. Certain trace elements, such as copper and manganese, possess antimicrobial properties that can help protect garlic plants from fungal diseases. Incorporating

micronutrient sprays into pest or disease management programs can provide an additional line of defence for garlic crops.

Best Practices for Foliar Feeding and Micronutrient Sprays in Garlic Farming:

To effectively incorporate foliar feeding and micronutrient sprays into garlic farming, consider the following best practices:

1. Timely Application: Apply foliar nutrients during periods of active garlic growth and when the plants are at their most receptive stage. Avoid applying foliar fertilizers during extreme temperature conditions or when the foliage is wet from rainfall or irrigation, as this may reduce the efficacy of the application.

2. Correct Nutrient Balance: Before applying foliar nutrients or micronutrient sprays, ensure that soil

nutrient levels are properly balanced through regular soil testing. This helps identify any existing nutrient deficiencies or excesses, allowing for more targeted and effective foliar feeding.

3. Consider Crop Stage: Different nutrients play varying roles at different stages of garlic growth. Adjust foliar feeding programs accordingly to meet the changing nutrient requirements of the garlic plants throughout their growth cycle. For example, nitrogen may be applied during vegetative growth, while potassium may be more critical during bulb development.

4. Follow Label Instructions: Read and adhere to the instructions provided on fertilizer labels or micronutrient spray products. Dilute the products according to the recommended rates and apply them using proper equipment to ensure uniform

coverage and minimize the risk of leaf burn or damage.

5. Monitor Nutrient Uptake: Regularly monitor plant nutrient status through tissue sampling or visual observation. This helps detect any deficiencies or excesses, enabling timely adjustments to the foliar feeding or micronutrient spray program.

6. Combine with Soil Amendments: Foliar feeding and micronutrient sprays should complement a comprehensive soil fertility program that includes soil amendments, organic matter applications, and balanced fertilizers. By integrating multiple approaches, growers can provide a comprehensive nutrient management plan to support optimal garlic growth and yield.

Chapter Five

Weed and Pest Control in Garlic Farming

5.1 Identifying and Managing Common Weeds in Garlic Fields

Weed management is an important aspect of garlic farming to ensure the optimal growth and yield of the crop. Weeds compete with garlic plants for essential resources such as nutrients, water, and sunlight, and can significantly reduce garlic yields if left uncontrolled. In addition, weeds can also act as hosts for pests and diseases, further impacting garlic production. Therefore, it is crucial for garlic farmers to properly identify and manage common weeds in garlic fields to implement effective weed and pest control measures. In this section, we will explore the identification of common weeds in garlic fields and share strategies for managing them effectively.

Identification of Common Weeds in Garlic Fields:

1. Grass Weeds - Grass weeds are some of the most common problematic weeds in garlic fields. They include species such as ryegrass, barnyard grass, crabgrass, and foxtail. Grass weeds can outcompete garlic plants and cause significant yield losses if not managed properly. They typically have long, slender leaves and a fibrous root system.

2. Broadleaf Weeds - Broadleaf weeds are another group of weeds commonly found in garlic fields. Examples include common lambsquarters, pigweed, chickweed, and dandelions. These weeds have broader leaves compared to grass weeds and can quickly colonize garlic fields if not controlled.

Broadleaf weeds often have taproots or fibrous root systems.

3. Sedges - Sedges are a type of weed that resembles grasses but can be distinguished by their triangular stems and three-ranked leaves. Common sedges found in garlic fields include yellow nutsedge and purple nutsedge. Sedges are particularly troublesome as they can spread rapidly and are difficult to control due to their extensive underground tuber systems.

4. Perennial Weeds - Perennial weeds are persistent and can pose a long-term challenge in garlic fields. Examples include Canada thistle, bindweed, and field bindweed. These weeds have deep root systems and are capable of regrowing year after year. Effective management of perennial weeds often requires a combination of cultural, mechanical, and chemical control methods.

Strategies for Managing Common Weeds in Garlic Fields:

a. Preventive Measures - Implementing preventive measures before planting garlic can help reduce weed pressure in the field. These include following fields before garlic planting, proper crop rotation, and maintaining clean machinery and equipment to prevent the introduction of weed seeds.

b. Cultural Control - Cultural practices play a crucial role in weed management in garlic fields. Some effective cultural control strategies include:

- Mulching: Applying organic mulch such as straw, hay, or wood chips around garlic plants can help suppress weed growth by blocking sunlight and reducing weed seed germination.

- Proper Spacing: Planting garlic bulbs at the recommended spacing allows the crop to compete more effectively with weeds and reduces weed establishment.
- Crop Rotation: Rotating garlic with non-host crops can disrupt weed life cycles and reduce weed populations over time.

  a. Mechanical Control - Mechanical weed control methods can be an effective way to manage weed populations in garlic fields. Some common mechanical control strategies include:

- Hand Weeding: Hand weeding is labour-intensive but can be an effective way to remove weeds from garlic fields, especially during the early stages when weed populations are relatively low.

- Cultivation: Careful cultivation using suitable tools, such as wheel hoes or sweeps, can help control weeds between rows while minimizing garlic plant damage. Timing is crucial to avoid weed interference and garlic bulb damage.
- Mowing or Cutting: Regular mowing or cutting of weeds in the garlic field can help prevent weed seed production and suppress weed growth.
  a. Chemical Control - Herbicides can be an effective tool for managing weeds in garlic fields when used judiciously and according to label instructions. It is essential to select herbicides that are registered for use in garlic and follow proper application rates and timings. Herbicides should be used as part of an integrated weed management approach and not as the sole method of weed control.

- Crop Vigor and Competitiveness - Healthy and vigorously growing garlic plants can better compete with weeds for resources. Good agronomic practices such as proper irrigation, balanced fertilization, and disease management can help promote crop vigor and improve competitiveness against weeds.

- Monitoring and Early Intervention - Regular monitoring of garlic fields is crucial to detect weed presence and take appropriate action. Early intervention, such as hand weeding or targeted herbicide application, can help prevent weeds from becoming established and reduce the overall weed population.

Integration of Weed Control Methods - Combining multiple weed control methods, such as cultural, mechanical, and chemical control, can provide the most effective and sustainable approach to weed management in garlic fields. Integrated weed management reduces reliance on any single method and helps prevent the development of herbicide-resistant weed populations.

5.2 Natural Weed Control Methods and Mulching

In garlic farming, natural weed control methods and mulching offer sustainable and effective ways to manage weeds and pests while reducing reliance on chemicals. These methods not only help control weed populations but also improve soil health, conserve water, and create a favourable environment for garlic crops. In this section, we will explore various natural weed control methods and the benefits of mulching for weed and pest control in garlic farming.

Natural Weed Control Methods:

1. Hand Weeding - Hand weeding remains one of the most basic and effective natural methods for controlling weeds in garlic fields. Regular inspection and manual removal of weeds help prevent their spread and reduce competition with garlic plants. Hand weeding is particularly useful during early growth stages when weed populations are small.

2. Mulching - Mulching with organic materials is a highly beneficial natural weed control method. Mulch helps suppress weed growth by blocking sunlight and preventing weed seed germination. Some effective mulching materials for garlic farming include straw, hay, wood chips, or dried leaves. Apply a layer of mulch around garlic plants, ensuring it does not come into direct contact with the stems or bulbs.

3. Cover Crops - Planting cover crops between garlic rows can help suppress weeds by utilizing available space and resources. Cover crops such as winter rye, oats, or clover can outcompete weeds and protect the soil from erosion. The cover crops can be mowed or tilled into the soil before garlic planting to provide organic matter and optimize weed suppression.

4. Flame Weeding - Flame weeding involves the use of propane burners to heat and kill weeds. It is an effective method for controlling young weeds and can be used along garlic rows or between rows. Flame weeding is best carried out during early weed growth stages to prevent weed competition without damaging garlic plants.

5. Vinegar-Based Herbicides - Vinegar-based herbicides, also known as acetic acid herbicides,

are natural alternatives to synthetic herbicides. These herbicides contain a high concentration of acetic acid, which has a desiccating effect on plant tissues. Vinegar-based herbicides can be effective when sprayed directly onto weeds. However, it's important to use caution when applying them to avoid contact with garlic plants, as these herbicides can damage desirable vegetation as well.

Benefits of Mulching for Weed and Pest Control:

Mulching provides multiple benefits for weed and pest control in garlic farming:

1. Weed Suppression - Mulching blocks sunlight and prevents weed seed germination, reducing weed competition with garlic plants. It helps to smother existing weeds and inhibits new weed growth, resulting in fewer weeds and less overall weed pressure.

2. Water Conservation - Mulching helps conserve soil moisture by reducing evaporation and minimizing water loss from the soil surface. By maintaining optimal soil moisture levels, mulching supports the growth and development of garlic plants while preventing weed growth.

3. Temperature Regulation - Mulch acts as an insulating layer, regulating soil temperature by keeping it cooler in hot weather and warmer in colder conditions. This temperature regulation helps optimize garlic plant growth while deterring weed seed germination.

4. Erosion Control - Mulch helps prevent soil erosion by protecting the soil surface from heavy rain or irrigation. It reduces the impact of water, preventing the displacement of soil particles and the loss of nutrients. By reducing erosion, mulching helps

maintain a stable soil environment for garlic plants and inhibits weed colonization.

5. Improved Soil Health - As organic mulch decomposes, it adds organic matter to the soil, improving its structure, fertility, and water-holding capacity. The addition of organic matter enhances soil health, promotes beneficial soil microorganisms, and contributes to a more favourable growing environment for garlic while suppressing weed growth.

6. Pest Prevention - Mulching can serve as a barrier against certain pests, including soil-borne pests such as nematodes. The mulch acts as a physical barrier that can prevent pests from reaching the garlic roots or feeding on the bulbs. Additionally, certain types of organic mulch, such as straw or wood chips, can host beneficial insects that help

control pests by attracting and providing habitat for natural predators.

Best Practices for Natural Weed Control Methods and Mulching:

To effectively utilize natural weed control methods and mulching in garlic farming, consider the following best practices:

1. Timing - Apply mulch after garlic plants have established themselves and reached a height of several inches. This helps prevent mulch from inhibiting garlic emergence and ensures that garlic plants have enough light to grow robustly.

2. Mulch Depth - Apply a layer of mulch around 2 to 4 inches thick to effectively suppress weed growth. A thicker layer can further inhibit weed germination and provide better weed control.

3. Weed-Free Area - Before applying mulch, remove existing weeds in the area to prevent them from growing through the mulch layer. Addressing weeds before mulching reduces the potential for weed competition and ensures more effective weed control.

4. Mulch Maintenance - Regularly monitor and maintain mulch throughout the garlic growing season. Replenish any areas where the mulch has thinned or decomposed to maintain effective weed suppression and other benefits.

5. Selecting Suitable Mulch - Choose organic mulch materials that are readily available, cost-effective, and suitable for the local conditions. Consider factors such as water retention, decomposition rate, and weed suppression capabilities when selecting mulching materials.

5.3 Integrated Pest Management (IPM) for Garlic

Integrated Pest Management (IPM) is a comprehensive approach to weed and pest control in garlic farming that combines various strategies to minimize the use of chemical pesticides while effectively managing pests. IPM focuses on preventing pest problems, monitoring pest populations, and utilizing a combination of cultural, biological, and chemical control methods when necessary. In this section, we will explore how IPM can be applied to garlic farming for weed and pest control.

Components of Integrated Pest Management (IPM):

1. Prevention and Monitoring - The first step in IPM is to prevent pest problems by implementing proactive measures. Garlic farmers should focus on maintaining healthy plants through good agronomic practices, such as proper irrigation, balanced nutrition, and optimal planting density. Regular

monitoring of garlic fields is also essential to detect pest infestations early and assess population levels.

2. Cultural Control - Cultural practices play a crucial role in preventing and managing pests in garlic farming. Some cultural control methods include crop rotation, sanitation, and proper field preparation. Crop rotation helps disrupt pest life cycles and reduces build-up of pests specific to garlic. Sanitation practices involve removing crop debris, which can harbor pests and diseases. Proper field preparation, such as plowing and shaping beds, can help reduce weed and pest pressure.

3. Biological Control - Biological control involves using natural enemies to suppress pest populations. This can include beneficial insects, such as parasitoids and predators, that feed on pests. Some beneficial

insects that can help control pests in garlic farming include ladybugs, lacewings, and parasitic wasps. Additionally, the use of microbial agents, such as beneficial bacteria or fungi, can be employed to suppress pests or pathogens.

4. Mechanical Control - Mechanical control methods involve physically removing pests or creating physical barriers. For weed control, mechanical methods include hand weeding, hoeing, or cultivation. For pest control, physical barriers like row covers or netting can be used to exclude pests from reaching the garlic plants.

5. Chemical Control - Although chemical control is not the primary focus of IPM, it can be used as a last resort if other methods fail to manage pest populations. When using chemical pesticides, it is important to select products that are specifically labeled for garlic and follow the label instructions

and safety precautions carefully. Integrated Pest Management aims to minimize the use of chemical pesticides by only using them when necessary and in a targeted manner.

Implementing Integrated Pest Management (IPM) for Garlic Farming:

1. Scouting and Monitoring - Regular field scouting and monitoring are critical components of IPM. Garlic farmers should routinely inspect their fields for signs of pests, including weeds, insects, and diseases. By monitoring pest populations, farmers can determine the severity of infestations and make informed decisions regarding pest control.

2. Identify and Assess Pest Problems - Once pests are identified, it is important to accurately identify the pest species and assess the potential damage they may cause. Some pest problems in garlic

farming include weed competition, bulb mites, onion thrips, or fungal diseases such as white rot or rust. Understanding the specific pests involved is crucial for determining the appropriate control measures.

3. Threshold Levels - Establishing threshold levels helps determine when pest populations have reached a point where action is necessary. Threshold levels vary depending on the pest and crop, and are usually based on scientific research or local recommendations. Garlic farmers should be aware of these thresholds and take action accordingly.

4. Utilize Cultural and Biological Control Methods - Cultural and biological control methods should be the primary focus of IPM in garlic farming. Implement proper cultural practices, including crop rotation, sanitation, and field preparation

techniques to reduce pest pressure. Additionally, encourage the presence and activity of beneficial insects by planting nectar-rich flowering plants near garlic fields.

5. Implement Mechanical Control Measures - Mechanical control methods, such as hand weeding, hoeing, or cultivation, can be used to manage weeds in garlic fields. Regularly remove weeds before they compete with garlic plants for nutrients, water, and sunlight. Mechanical methods can also help physically remove pests from the field.

6. Chemical Control as a Last Resort - If pest populations exceed threshold levels and cultural, biological, and mechanical methods are insufficient, chemical control can be used as a last resort. When selecting chemical pesticides, choose products labelled for garlic and follow the label

instructions carefully. Apply pesticides during the recommended stage of pest development and consider the impact on beneficial insects, adjacent crops, and the environment.

7. Record Keeping and Evaluation - Maintain records of pest monitoring, control measures implemented, and their effectiveness. Regularly evaluate the success of IPM practices in managing weeds and pests in garlic farming. These records can help identify patterns, adjust strategies, and improve future pest management efforts.

5.4 Common Garlic Pests and Disease Prevention

Garlic farming is susceptible to various pests and diseases that can significantly impact crop yield and quality if left unmanaged. Implementing effective pest and disease prevention strategies is crucial for successful garlic production. By adopting proactive measures, garlic farmers can minimise the occurrence and severity of pest and disease infestations, leading to healthier plants and increased productivity. In this section, we will explore common garlic pests and diseases and discuss prevention methods for weed and pest control in garlic farming.

Common Garlic Pests:

1. Onion Thrips (Thrips tabaci) – Thrips are tiny insects that feed on garlic leaves and bulbs, causing stunted growth, leaf and bulb discoloration, and premature drying. Implementing proactive measures such as regular monitoring, physical barriers, and the use of beneficial insects like predatory mites can help control thrips populations.

2. Bulb Mites (Rhizoglyphus spp.) – Bulb mites feed on garlic bulbs, leading to discolored, rotting, and shriveled cloves. To prevent infestations, practice proper field sanitation, avoid overcrowding of

plants, and use disease-free bulb seed stock. Additionally, avoid excessive irrigation as moist conditions favor mite development.

3. Nematodes (Meloidogyne spp.) – Nematodes are microscopic soil-dwelling worms that attack plant roots, leading to stunted growth, wilting, and reduced yield. Crop rotation with non-host plants, such as grains or legumes, can help reduce nematode populations. Additionally, practicing good weed control and maintaining optimal soil moisture levels can reduce nematode damage.

4. Garlic Maggot (Hylemya spp.) – Garlic maggots are the larvae of small flies that feed on garlic roots, causing wilting, yellowing, and eventual death of plants. Crop rotation and the use of beneficial insects, such as parasitic wasps, can help control garlic maggot populations. Additionally, removing

and destroying infested plants can limit their spread.

5. Wireworms (Agriotes spp.) – Wireworms are the larvae of click beetles that burrow into garlic bulbs, resulting in hollowed-out cloves. To prevent wireworm infestations, practice crop rotation with non-host plants, such as grasses, to target and eliminate wireworm populations.

Common Garlic Diseases:

1. White Rot (Sclerotium cepivorum) – White rot is a fungal disease that affects garlic plants, causing yellowing, wilting, and rotting of leaves and bulbs. Preventative measures include using disease-free bulb seed stock, crop rotation, and avoiding fields where white rot has been present before. Proper field drainage and sanitation practices are also crucial for preventing white rot.

2. Downy Mildew (Peronospora destructor) – Downy mildew is a common fungal disease that affects garlic leaves, causing yellow patches, curling, and eventual death of foliage. Planting resistant garlic varieties, practicing proper irrigation methods, and improving air circulation through proper spacing can help prevent downy mildew.

3. Rust (Puccinia spp.) – Rust is a fungal disease that appears as orange or reddish-brown patches on garlic leaves. To prevent rust, maintain proper plant spacing to improve air circulation, avoid overhead irrigation, and promptly remove and destroy infected plant material.

4. Botrytis Rot (Botrytis spp.) – Botrytis rot is a fungal disease that primarily affects garlic bulbs, causing gray mold, rotting, and fuzzy growth. Thorough field sanitation, proper curing of harvested garlic, and

efficient moisture management in storage are essential for preventing botrytis rot.

Prevention and Management Strategies:

To prevent and manage common garlic pests and diseases, garlic farmers should consider the following strategies:

1. Starting with Disease-Free Bulb Seed Stock – Use certified disease-free garlic bulbs as seed stock to prevent the introduction and spread of pests and diseases onto the farm.

2. Crop Rotation – Rotate garlic crops with non-host plants to break pest and disease life cycles and reduce the build-up of pathogens and pests in the soil. Avoid planting garlic or other Allium crops in the same field year after year.

3. Good Field Sanitation – Clear the fields of crop debris, as they can harbour pests and diseases. Properly dispose of infected crop residue to prevent the spread of pathogens.

4. Optimal Spacing and Planting Density – Provide adequate spacing between garlic plants to improve airflow, reduce humidity, and minimize the spread of diseases. Avoid overcrowding, as it creates a favourable environment for pests and diseases to thrive.

5. Proper Irrigation and Drainage – Avoid overwatering, as excessive moisture can lead to disease development and attract pests. Implement proper irrigation techniques that ensure adequate but not excessive moisture for garlic plants. Maintain proper field drainage to prevent waterlogging.

6. Weed Control – Prevent weed competition by implementing proper weed control measures. Weeds can harbour pests and diseases, adversely affecting garlic plants.

7. Use of Beneficial Insects – Promote the presence and activity of beneficial insects, such as predatory mites or parasitic wasps, which help control pest populations naturally. Avoid excessive use of broad-spectrum pesticides that can harm beneficial insects.

8. Regular Monitoring – Frequent field scouting and monitoring allow early detection of pest and disease infestations. Prompt action can be taken to prevent their spread and minimise damage.

9. Proper Harvesting and Post-Harvest Handling – Handle garlic bulbs with care during harvesting to avoid damage that may provide entry points for disease pathogens. Properly cure harvested garlic

to increase its shelf life and reduce the risk of post-harvest diseases.

Chapter Six

Harvesting and Curing Garlic

6.1 Signs of Garlic Maturity and Readiness for Harvest

Knowing when to harvest garlic is crucial to ensure that the bulbs reach their maximum size and flavor potential. Harvesting garlic too early can result in small, underdeveloped bulbs, while leaving it in the ground for too long can cause the cloves to separate and sprout, reducing their quality. By understanding the signs of garlic maturity and readiness for harvest, garlic farmers can harvest their crop at the optimal time for the best results.

Here are the key signs to look for to determine when garlic is mature and ready for harvest:

1. Leaf Browning and Drying - As the garlic bulbs mature, the lower leaves of the plant will start to

turn yellow and dry out. This is a natural process as the plant redirects its energy towards bulb development. It is important to note that some leaf discoloration is normal during the garlic's growth cycle. However, when about 60-70% of the leaves have turned yellow and dried up, it is usually a good indicator that the garlic is nearing maturity.

2. Stem Loosening - Another sign of garlic maturity is the loosening of the stem from the bulb or the appearance of empty spaces between the stem and the bulb. This can often be felt when gently squeezing the stem near the base of the bulb. A loosened stem indicates that the garlic has reached its full growth potential and is ready for harvest.

3. Papery Skin Formation - When garlic is approaching maturity, the outer skin of the bulbs will undergo changes. The thin and papery outer skin will become tighter and more firmly attached to the

cloves. This protective layer helps preserve the garlic bulbs during the curing process and extends their shelf life. If the skin is still loose and not tightly formed around the cloves, the garlic may not be fully mature and should be left to grow further.

4. Bulb Size - Garlic bulbs should be plump and well-formed before harvesting. The individual cloves should have filled out, and the overall size of the bulb should be substantial. Mature garlic bulbs usually have a diameter of about 1.5 to 2 inches (3.8 to 5 centimeters) or more, depending on the variety grown. Smaller bulbs may still have potential for growth and should be left in the ground for a little longer.

5. Cloves Filling Out the Skin - When garlic is ready for harvest, the cloves within the bulb will fill out their skins completely. The spaces between the cloves should be tight, and there should be no

noticeable gaps or air pockets. Fully developed cloves indicate that the bulbs have reached maturity and are ready to be harvested.

To determine if garlic is mature and ready for harvest, it is recommended to perform a "flash test" on a few bulbs. Carefully dig up a small portion of the garlic bed and gently remove a bulb for evaluation. If the bulb meets the criteria of leaf browning and drying, stem loosening, papery skin formation, and filled-out cloves, it is a good indication that the rest of the garlic crop is also mature and ready for harvest.

Once garlic is harvested, it is important to promptly move on to the curing process. Curing involves drying the harvested garlic bulbs in a well-ventilated and dry area for a period of 2 to 4 weeks. This helps remove excess moisture, develop the characteristic flavor, and extend the shelf life of the garlic. During curing, the plant's nutrients are directed from the leaves to the bulbs, helping to enhance the garlic's taste and texture.

To properly cure garlic, follow these steps:

1. Brush off Excess Soil - Gently remove any loose dirt or soil from the harvested bulbs, being careful not to damage the outer skin.

2. Leave the Stems and Leaves Intact - Keep the bulbs attached to their stems and leave the dried leaves intact. These provide a natural protective layer during curing.

3. Create a Well-Ventilated Environment - Hang the garlic in bunches or arrange them in single layers on mesh racks or screens in a well-ventilated area.

Make sure the environment is dry, with good air circulation and limited exposure to direct sunlight.

4. Maintain Optimal Conditions - The curing area should have temperatures between 70 to 80°F (21 to 27°C) and relative humidity levels of around 60% to 70%. Avoid exposure to excessive moisture or high humidity as this can lead to mold or rot.

5. Regularly Inspect and Remove Defective Bulbs - Check on the curing garlic periodically and remove any bulbs showing signs of mold, rot, or damage. This will prevent the spread of disease and ensure the quality of the remaining bulbs.

6.2 Harvesting Techniques for Green Garlic and Bulb Garlic

Garlic can be harvested in two different stages, depending on the desired use and market demand. Green garlic, also known as baby garlic or spring garlic, refers to garlic plants that are harvested early when the bulbs are still immature and the tops are green and tender. Bulb garlic, on the other hand, is harvested when the bulbs have fully matured and are ready for curing and storage. Understanding the different harvesting techniques for green garlic and bulb garlic is essential to ensure optimal flavour and quality.

Harvesting Techniques for Green Garlic:

Green garlic is harvested before the bulbs have fully matured, usually during the early stages of growth when the plants have thin, tender, green tops. Green garlic is highly valued for its mild, fresh flavour, and is often used in culinary preparations such as salads, stir-fries, and soups.

To harvest green garlic, follow these techniques:

a. Timing: Green garlic can be harvested approximately 60 to 90 days after planting, depending on the variety.

Harvesting too early may result in small, underdeveloped bulbs, while waiting too long could lead to overly mature and pungent bulbs. Monitor the growth of the garlic plants closely and harvest when the tops are still green and tender.

b. Loosening the Soil: Gently loosen the soil around the base of the garlic plant using a fork or trowel. Be cautious not to damage the garlic bulbs or roots in the process.

c. Lifting the Clumps: Carefully lift the entire clump of green garlic out of the ground, ensuring that the bulbs and roots remain intact. Shake off excess soil but avoid removing too much dirt, as it helps protect the tender roots and bulbs during handling.

d. Trimming and Cleaning: Trim off the roots, leaving a small portion attached to the bulbs. Trim any damaged or discoloured leaves, and remove any loose outer layers around the bulbs. Rinse the green garlic under cool water to remove any remaining soil.

e. Storage and Usage: Green garlic has a short shelf life and should be used soon after harvesting. Store the green garlic in the refrigerator in a plastic bag or container for up to one week. The tender green tops can be chopped and used in various culinary applications, while the bulbs can be sliced and added to dishes for a milder garlic flavour.

Harvesting Techniques for Bulb Garlic:

Bulb garlic is harvested when the bulbs have fully matured and are at their optimal size and flavour for long-term storage. The bulbs are allowed to develop fully in the ground before they are lifted and cured. Harvested bulbs can be used for cooking, planting as seed stock for the next season, or sold to the market.

To harvest bulb garlic, follow these techniques:

a. Timing: Bulb garlic is typically harvested around mid-summer, about 3 to 4 weeks after the foliage has started to die back. The leaves should have turned brown or yellow, indicating that the bulbs have reached maturity and are ready for curing.

b. Loosening the Soil: Gently loosen the soil around the base of the garlic plants using a fork or shovel. Take care not to damage the bulbs during the digging process.

c. Lifting the Bulbs: Lift the garlic bulbs out of the ground using your hands or a garden fork. Start by lifting the bulbs slightly so that the remaining soil falls off naturally. Avoid pulling or twisting the plants, as this can cause damage to the bulbs.

d. Cleaning and Curing: Gently brush off any excess soil from the bulbs, being careful not to remove the papery outer skin. Do not wash the bulbs, as this can introduce excess moisture that may interfere with the curing process. Bundle the harvested garlic into groups of 6 to 12 bulbs, and hang them in a dry, well-ventilated area to cure for 2 to 4 weeks. This curing process allows the bulbs to dry and develop a stronger flavor.

e. Trimming and Storage: After the garlic bulbs have cured, trim off the dried leaves and roots. Leave the papery outer skin intact, as it helps protect the bulbs during storage. Store the cured bulbs in a cool, dry, and dark location with good air circulation. Properly cured and stored bulb garlic can last several months, depending on the variety.

f. Seed Stock Selection: When saving bulbs for planting as seed stock, choose the largest, healthiest bulbs from your harvest. These bulbs will have the best potential for producing robust and flavorful garlic in the following growing season.

6.3 Curing Garlic: Drying, Cleaning, and Storing Methods

Curing garlic is a critical step in the garlic production process. Curing allows the garlic to dry, develop its flavour, and extend its shelf life. Proper drying, cleaning, and storage methods are essential to protect the quality and longevity of the harvested garlic. Here are some effective techniques for curing garlic.

Drying Garlic

After harvesting, garlic bulbs should be dried to remove excess moisture and enhance the flavour. Here are some drying techniques for garlic:

a. Hanging Garlic: Hang harvested garlic in a well-ventilated area using twine or netting. Allow the bulbs to hang with plenty of space between them, making sure that they are not touching or overlapping. A dry, breezy location is ideal for drying garlic, such as an attic or garage.

b. Air Drying Racks: Lay garlic bulbs on wire mesh racks for drying in a dry and well-ventilated location. Place the racks on blocks or stands, allowing ample air circulation around the bulbs. Air-drying racks allow maximum airflow, ensuring optimal drying of the garlic bulbs.

c. Sun Drying: Sun drying is a traditional method of drying garlic in some regions. Place the harvested garlic bulbs on an elevated surface in direct sunlight, making sure to rotate them every few hours to ensure even drying. Avoid exposing garlic to sunlight for too long, as it can cause discoloration and decrease its flavour intensity.

Cleaning Garlic

Cleaning garlic bulbs after drying removes any dirt or debris, and prepares the garlic bulbs for storage. Here are some cleaning techniques for garlic:

a. Dry Brushing: Use a dry brush to gently rub off any excess dirt or debris from the garlic bulbs. Avoid using water or other cleaning agents as this can add moisture which may damage the garlic bulbs during storage.

b. Compressed Air: Use compressed air to blow off any debris from the garlic bulbs. Compressed air is ideal for those who prefer not to use a brush.

Storing Garlic

Properly storing cured garlic ensures that the cloves retain their full flavor and last for several months. Here are some storing techniques for garlic:

a. Cool and Dry Location: Store garlic bulbs in a cool and dry location, preferably between 32 and 50°F (0-10°C). A dark pantry or basement is ideal for this purpose.

b. Ventilated Containers: Store garlic bulbs in mesh bags or wire baskets to allow air circulation. Proper ventilation helps prevent moisture buildup and extends the shelf life of the garlic bulbs.

c. Avoid Moisture and Humidity: Garlic bulbs should be kept away from excessive moisture and humidity. Avoid storing garlic in the refrigerator, as the moisture can cause mold and sprouting. Garlic bulbs should also be kept away from any sources of heat or direct sunlight.

d. Seed Stock Selection: Save the largest and healthiest garlic bulbs for planting as seed stock for the following growing season. Selecting the best bulbs ensures the production of quality garlic in the next harvest.

6.4 Preventing Post-Harvest Diseases and Spoilage

Preventing post-harvest diseases and spoilage is crucial to ensuring the quality and longevity of harvested and cured garlic. Garlic is susceptible to various diseases and storage issues that can reduce its value and marketability.

Implementing proper preventive measures and storage techniques can help minimize these problems. Here are some effective methods for preventing post-harvest diseases and spoilage in garlic.

Harvesting at the Right Time

Harvest garlic when it has reached its optimal maturity. Waiting too long can lead to overripe bulbs that are prone to spoilage and disease. Harvesting too early can result in underdeveloped bulbs that have shorter shelf life. Monitor the garlic plants closely and harvest when the tops have withered and about 40 to 60% of the foliage has dried down.

Proper Handling and Sanitation

Handle garlic with care during and after harvest to prevent physical damage and the introduction of pathogens. Follow these guidelines for proper handling and sanitation:

a. Use Clean Equipment: Use clean tools and containers when handling garlic to prevent the spread of diseases and contaminants. Clean and sanitize equipment regularly to minimize the risk of contamination.

b. Remove Excess Soil: Gently remove excess soil from the garlic bulbs after harvest, taking care not to damage the protective outer layers. Excess soil can harbor disease-causing organisms that could lead to spoilage.

c. Avoid Damaging Bulbs: Be cautious during handling to avoid bruising or cutting the garlic bulbs, as damaged bulbs are more susceptible to disease.

d. Dispose of Infected Bulbs: If any bulbs show signs of disease or rot, remove and discard them immediately to prevent the spread of pathogens.

Curing Garlic Properly

Proper drying and curing are essential to removing excess moisture from garlic bulbs, preventing the growth and spread of fungi and bacteria. Refer to section 6.3 for detailed techniques on drying, cleaning, and storing garlic.

Storage Conditions

The storage conditions play a critical role in preventing post-harvest diseases and spoilage. Here are some measures to consider:

a. Optimal Temperature and Humidity: Garlic is best stored in a cool and dry environment with a temperature range of

32 to 50°F (0-10°C) and a humidity level of 60-70%. Avoid storing garlic in areas with high humidity or fluctuating temperatures, as these conditions can promote the growth of mould and sprouting.

b. Good Air Circulation: Proper air circulation helps prevent the buildup of moisture and reduces the risk of fungal growth. Store garlic in mesh bags or wire baskets that allow for ventilation.

c. Regular Inspection: Regularly inspect stored garlic for any signs of spoilage, such as mould, rot, or sprouting. Remove any affected bulbs promptly to prevent the spread of disease.

Seed Stock Management

Proper management of seed stock is crucial to avoid introducing diseases into the next season's crop. Implement the following practices:

a. Selection of Healthy Bulbs: Choose the largest, healthiest garlic bulbs for seed stock. Select bulbs that are free from disease, rot, or damage, as they are more likely to produce healthy plants in the next growing season.

b. Isolation and Quarantine: Isolate newly acquired or suspicious garlic bulbs from the main stock to prevent the potential spread of diseases. Monitor isolated bulbs closely for signs of infection before introducing them into the main seed stock.

c. Crop Rotation: Practice crop rotation to minimize the build-up of garlic-specific diseases in the soil. Avoid planting garlic in the same location year after year.

Regular Cleaning and Sanitization

Maintain good hygiene by regularly cleaning and sanitizing storage areas, tools, and equipment used for handling garlic. Sanitize storage containers, racks, and other equipment using a solution of bleach or sanitizing agents to kill any pathogens present.

Conclusion

Garlic farming requires knowledge, skill, and dedication to be successful. Whether you are an experienced farmer looking to diversify your crops or a beginner looking for a profitable venture, growing and selling garlic can be a rewarding endeavour. This practical guide has covered the key aspects of garlic farming, from preparing the soil and selecting the right varieties to planting, nurturing, and harvesting the crop.

By understanding the specific needs of garlic plants, farmers can provide optimal growing conditions and ensure healthy plant development. Proper soil preparation, including proper drainage and the addition of organic matter, sets the foundation for a successful garlic crop. Selecting suitable garlic varieties based on regional climate, taste preference, and market demand is crucial for maximizing profit potential.

The guide has also covered various cultivation techniques, such as planting methods, fertilization, irrigation, and weed and pest management. Implementing sustainable and organic farming practices not only ensures the long-term health of the garlic crop but also adds value to the end product, appealing to health-conscious consumers.

Harvesting and curing garlic in the right manner preserve the flavor and quality of the bulbs, extending their shelf life and marketability. Drying, cleaning, and proper storage techniques protect the harvested garlic from post-harvest diseases and spoilage, allowing farmers to maintain the freshness and value of the crop.

To maximize profits from selling garlic, farmers need to consider marketing strategies, including identifying target markets, building relationships with buyers, and exploring direct-to-consumer channels such as farmers markets and online platforms. Taking advantage of the growing demand for organic and specialty garlic will further enhance the profitability of the garlic farming business.

However, success in garlic farming goes beyond the technical aspects. It requires a genuine passion for the crop and a strong work ethic. Diligence, attention to detail, and adaptability are essential qualities for garlic farmers. Continuous learning, staying updated on industry trends, and networking with other farmers and experts contribute to the long-term viability and profitability of the garlic farming business.

Garlic farming is undoubtedly an art that requires patience, knowledge, and continuous improvement. As a farmer delves into the world of garlic cultivation, they discover the unique nuances and challenges associated with this crop.

But with dedication, perseverance, and a commitment to quality, garlic farming can be a rewarding and profitable venture.

As garlic farmers embark on their journey, embracing the practices outlined in this guide and applying their own creativity and expertise will pave the way for a thriving garlic farming business. From the satisfaction of nurturing the plants through each stage of growth to the joy of seeing customers delighted with their flavorful garlic, the art of garlic farming offers not only financial returns but also a deep sense of fulfillment.

www.ingramcontent.com/pod-product-compliance
Lightning Source LLC
Chambersburg PA
CBHW071205290526
45796CB00008B/149